HEARTBREAK TREE

poems

HEARTBREAK TREE

poems

Pauletta Hansel

MADVILLE
PUBLISHING

Lake Dallas, Texas

FIRST EDITION

Requests for permission to reprint or reuse material
from this work should be sent to:

Permissions
Madville Publishing
PO Box 358
Lake Dallas, TX 75065

Cover Design: Jacqueline Davis
Cover Art: painting by Angelyn DeBord

ISBN:
978-1-948692-88-5 paperback
978-1-948692-89-2 ebook
Library of Congress Control Number: 2021941186

TABLE OF CONTENTS

I.

II.

III.

IV.

For RGH,
a mother to these words

I.

STORY

I don't mean to be ungrateful.
I was bred for wanting more, the way
a racehorse is bred for the win's scent.
Those impossible legs like winged twigs
that will snap in a high wind.
What moves us onward is the same,
sometimes, as what breaks us to the ground.
Here's a story about my grandfather
that I don't like to tell,
how he found a WWII deserter's bundle
tucked inside a cave,
how he kept the money, then turned the guy in
for a $15 reward.
I'm not saying our people weren't hungry.
We were always hungry.
I'm not saying who my grandfather was
is who I am.
What my mother wanted
was to be far away
from where she started.
What my father wanted
was to begin again.
I'm telling you
the hardest thing
I've ever had to do
is to stop wanting
what I already have.

Letter to Myself, 15

When are we going to see each other at last?
  —Henri Michaux, "I Am Writing to You from a Far-Off Country"

Listen, girl,
you are
despite yourself,
becoming,
not become.
I know you think there's safety
in the fused bone, woman grown.
There is no safety
in your body, stretched lean
into the world, only skin
between you and your longing,
and skin can be broken,
and you can be broken.
You are.
We are. Girl,
listen, I say,
but I know you will not.
My words are a swirl
picked up by the wind,
brought back
to me.

DIRT

What people in town remember about my family's home
was the dirt in the fenced front yard where no grass
could stay grown, worn down by the feet of the kids
Mom kept in the daycare where I worked too
the summer I was 15,
in my shorts and tank top,
sitting out on the rock wall that bisected
the dirt of the yard from the dirt of the driveway.
Once an old woman driving stopped—I don't know how old
is old, maybe the old I am now, older than dirt—
carved crevices around her mouth,
to tell me she once had a waist like mine,
steep sloping down,
though her ass sat up higher.

> I have been thinking about dirt,
> or maybe the rock along the road
> I never noticed I'd noticed growing up there,
> sandstone and shale striated with coal
> that always looked wet even in summer,
> grass a paler brown than the dirt
> which, depending on where in the county you were,
> might be a gravelly sandy stony silty loam.

Maybe she said buttocks.
Probably she said butt.
I didn't know what to say to her.
I had nothing
to say.

On the road out of town,
KY 15 to the Parkway to the highway—
an hour to there and you're almost to Lexington
where there's something to do, not sit
surrounded by kids and old
and dirt (rough broken mountainous
deeply dissected).

I didn't know that I knew
how the farther you got up the road
the coal is gone,
there's clay in the rock
and the grass is greener,
I mean, really it is,
on the other side.

The Road

There is one patch of Route 15, just north
of what was home, where whatever weather is,
there is more of it—cloudburst, blizzard, smear
of sun that finds its way through needle eye
of mountain. You've pulled the tangled thread
of road with you this far. Go on. No one
waits, hand up to curtain listening for your
graveled turn. There's only past throwing
its shadow on the lane that sends you back
toward what is gone. Your eyes will soon adjust.
When did you know it's not enough
to carry splintered pieces underneath your skin?
Home is the place you must choose again.

Home Is the Place Where,
When You Have to Go There,
You Only Think About How to Get Out

Busted-up doll heads where the canned goods used to be.
Sunsteeped, hillbuckled sidewalks, and everybody
just looks tired. Nobody cares
this is where your mother used to buy her meat.
The houses you lived in plowed under,
moles scuttle through plumbing cracked with black dirt and roots.
Nobody cares about your old woman body
grown on the bones of the girl who walked these streets.
Everybody has their own worn bones.
Everybody remembers you, sort of.
The newspaperman calls you by your mother's name.
You can't remember the name
of who you sat next to in math class or whose backseat
you crawled out of nights, the river fog
so dense you came home hair and misplaced clothes
all damp and smelling like mountain. Nobody cares
you know this town by what is gone, stench
of grease spilled from the closed pool hall, mailbox on the corner
where the boys sprawled, pelvises jutted out to block your path.
You pull up your car too close to the high curb
somebody told you was made for hitching horses.
Nobody had any horses.

STORY

My mother said
she never asked again
who her oldest brother's
father was.

Granny didn't want
to talk about it.
That's all we needed
to know.

So I made stories
in my head
of someone kinder
than my grandpa,

his lips not folded thin
inside a nighttime scruff
of peppered gray.
I wanted that comfort for her,

if not in life, in memory
of a silken tangle of flesh
hidden between
tall rows of corn

back in Virginia
where her people stayed.
She never went back home,
not even after Grandpa died,

and finally she cut off
her waist-length hair, let her
daughter give her a home perm,
soft curls around her neck.

Years later,
almost everybody dead,
my aunt told me.
That old story.

A widowed father
stumble-drunk,
grizzling himself
into his daughter's bed.

Her name was Etta.
Before I knew her, ten children
had torn through that secret place
her father had claimed.

Poem Written While Contemplating a Newly Dug Southern Kentucky Grave

Neither born nor buried in such bright, heavy earth,
my mother, in between,
found a patch of her own and claimed it,
tamed it with horse shit and other black offerings
night after night as the sun went down behind a rise
so gentle she would hardly call it a hill,
much less a mountain. She knew
her mountains.
The shadows they made.
Here, only hers bent and rose, bent again
to make the bed her lilies would rise from.
Come fall she would press her small foot hard
against the spade's square edge,
push it deep through the layers of soil
to fling at my feet a pale, dangled cluster
I carried north, clay still clinging
to the roots. My mother
is ash now, her garden mowed over
and sown with someone else's seed.
By my door her lilies,
streaked red as turned clay.

For Beauty

I've seen beauty in Harlan / in the trailing arbutus... [but] beauty / is a
stranger / to the coal camps...
　　—Don West

Ground laurel, mayflower, trailing
its pink-tipped blooms
in the month of my father's birth.
Epigaea repens "upon the earth."
Arbutus "thee only do I love"
in the language of flowers, and he,
in his way, stayed true
to the ground he grew on.

My father always had to have the mountains in his sight.
No matter the trails of his sorrowing, restless mind,
his feet stayed planted
in mountain dirt.

> *"Trailing arbutus is very difficult to*
> *establish and perpetuate. It will not tolerate*
> *disturbance, is extremely susceptible to*
> *failure... even in good conditions."*

From him I learned
you could love what you also hate

> *gaunt-eyed, gulp down, everlasting*
> *grime and dirt*
> *and digging*

But beauty is never
a stranger.

JOY

When we finally sprung my father from the hospital
after days spent staring at the cardio unit's
cinderblock walls the color of nothing
good, his joy could not be contained.
Every meal he ate was the best he'd ever had.
I worried, at first, that my mother would feel slighted
by his ecumenical praise—the biscuits on the buffet line
at the Golden Corral no less holy than hers. But she knew
better than I how to savor his delights.
As we traveled the back roads from doctor to home,
he asked at every turn,
Have you ever seen a spring as beautiful as this,
the red of that maple, the washed denim sky?

I Take My Mother with Me Everywhere

In dream,
we are going to Alaska, but she doesn't

have any boots. She reminds me—
the lake she has always wanted

to see, southern waves lapping a green shore.
But we are going to Alaska

where beneath the lichen and moss
the land is forever frozen,

permanently impermeable,
as she is.

THE STEPMOTHER'S LAMENT

A mother, discarded,
is not gone.
She lives on,
marrow in the bones
of the daughter,
and the daughter,
too, still occupies
the organs of the body
once inhabited—
a fetal cell or two
or ten, pink within
the liver,
the hollow atrium,
the enflamed spleen.
I am telling you
the sentence is life.

Not so, my dear,
my once-upon-a-time,
my foundling girl,
my darling,
for you and me.
The pages of the tale
we were, slammed shut
and flung behind you.
I have no way but words
to sing you back
into the story
composed,
not flesh,
but choice
and chance.
Tell me,
what am I
supposed to do
with all this love?

Returned, Addressee Unknown

Friend, am I writing to you or am I writing to us, the girls we were, never two parts of a whole, but bound, somehow, by proximity and whatever else, unnamed? You were a redbud tree, lightning-struck, still standing. Blossoms sparking from the split— would they leaf and branch and grow? I made a nest inside the wound and flew away, flew away before it closed, me in it. Oh, how you'd hate these words. I was always just a little or a lot too precious for you. You were the rutted gravel road up the holler to the house; I was the car's scraped chassis. And I loved you. You loved me. Admit it. Those late-night vodka phone calls all those years ago; you'd wake me up, just because you knew I'd always answer. Why did they stop? Who abandoned who, that's what I want to know. And now? You are a dry-stone wall along the edge of scrubby woods that used to be a plowed field. And I am somewhere else, remembering.

STORY

When I was a kid
and lived just a county or two
up Kentucky Route 15 from that place
my mother once called home,
Granny would come from there
and help Mom pick the beetles from her roses,
tell her, if she'd not gone and got herself too fine
to keep some chickens,
there'd be no beetles here to pick.

But we weren't the sort of family
that circled back to what got left behind,
and though it's true that home
is what I always called
whatever hill town
my parents were in,
until they weren't,
home got boxed up
in a moving van from time to time,
houses and towns discarded,
snakeskin by the side of the road.

So later, when my granny told me
what she thought I already knew,
that I didn't live up North,
I only worked there,
I set her straight:
I will never move back home.

Some Facts about Home

1. The writing spider, AKA *argiope aurantia*, has developed several responses to predators, such as dropping off the web or retreating to its periphery.

2. The writing spider does not live in very dense location clusters like other orb spiders; she keeps a clean orderly web in comparison to their cluttered series of webs built and abandoned.

3. She can oscillate her web vigorously while she remains firmly attached in the center.

4. In a nightly ritual, she consumes the circular interior part of the web and then rebuilds it each morning with fresh new silk.

5. Spider webs are peculiar. Sometimes you see them; sometimes you don't. It's not necessarily because you're too close or too far; it's the angle, the quality of light.

Kanawha

Today's poem
is a river I write
in my head as I walk,
my feet in the feet of these lines.
Don't try to say its name
unless you've lived here.
I don't live here
anymore and the waters
don't carry the coal.
But the river still smells
of leaving and gone,
and along the flood wall
graffiti remembers
when Logan ♡ Steel.

It snows across the mountains

of my homeland,
snow over the green hills,
the trickling creekbeds, black rivers,
the honeysuckled banks, snow
over the August mountains,
over kudzu climbing
bent guardrails, ironweed purpling
the spent fields, snow
over the rusting tipples, the slashed hills,
their seams of coal slicking
through sandstone and shale,
over barns shorn down to their timber,
snow over empty schools
and shiny new clinics,
over steepled churches
and the flat-roofed Walmarts.
In my dream
it snows ash
and we dance
in our yards and in the parking lots,
ash, and we spill
out into our streets,
down the rutted paths beneath the bridges,
and to the road-sliced ridge,
knowing it is ash
and knowing
it is still beautiful—
this falling snow.

II.

Dear Moon

could you see it too?
dark scratch of birds
across your morning face
before you turned
from me.

Morning, Loretto Motherhouse, Late November

Wasp, old friend
from yesterday, wakes too
with the sun, first a wide swath of silk
draped against the far Knobs,
now a pulsing orb
I lean away from in my chair
to save my sight.
The wasp navigates the screen
that keeps him from flight
and death, come evening
frost that has already chilled
the leaves from the sycamore
where dark birds alight, then swoop
as in one gathered breath
away. O wasp!
Your careful crawl toward
blaze of death from which,
for all my pretty words,
I will not save you.

AFTER

Where does fear go when it dies—
no, that's not the right question,
it was never fear who lay
beneath bleached sheets, caged eyes wild,
then not. Now fear's talons have
nowhere to land. Mother's safe
in ground. Above, I circle.

Postcard from Age 60

Most mornings I unspool the knotted rope of me
into cool water, trying to dip down
into gratitude. My sinking body
in its nylon suit still moves as I tell it to,
the lift and push of limbs across the length of pool.
Mother, some days I even remember to thank
the ache that lives at the base of my spine, too,
for how it lifts me buoyant to this place of ease.
I am trying to believe it is not the weight,
but how we carry what we're given that bends
us down, or lets us float awhile, suspended
in these years between the gathering up
and letting go. Mother, I am trying
to let go, but not of everything, a soft
loosening of my clench upon this world
I entered through your body.

STORY

Have I ever told you my mother
canceled her newspaper subscription
when for the second time that ice-swathed winter
delivery was delayed? I think about this
while my husband labors to repair
on my computer those things invisible
I never knew I needed till they failed me.
And how I wake at night,
the chatter at the open window
of my brain—*she did, he said, they never will*—
My father held his grudges close,
poor substitute for love
his alcoholic father never turned his way.
When hurt is all that's handed down
you learn to claim it.
And so, I see you, friend,
inside the poem you sent me,
kneeling in your spring damp garden,
gloves on your quick hands.
You pull leaves from last year's
Lenten roses, looking for
the middle way my family never found—
to let it live, what's tender green inside;
to let them go before they cut too deep,
those jagged bits
of what's already gone.

Heartbreak Tree

The magnolia—bud, blossom, decay
all on one gnarled branch.

In the nursing home,
my mother asks, "Do you ever
shut your eyes and wonder,
whatever happened to *me*?"

PATTERN

My mother never followed a pattern
exactly as laid out
thin as snakeskin on the kitchen table.

It was the only time I ever saw her make a mess.
Days later, she would still be sweeping
straggled slivers of the dress

that my sister or I already wore.
Ours never looked exactly like the ones
beneath the label—Butterick, McCall.

She knew to bias cut the skirt
to skim our roundness,
add a row of stitches to the bust

we had yet to acquire.
I can't recall that either of us
ever thanked her

then. We wanted store bought, even though
she showed us how those flimsy things
came from the washer stretched and frayed.

Neither of us took her Singer
when she died.
My sister took some of the patterns

for the pictures, though the papers
never folded flat inside,
the way they'd come.

I still have the last dress she made me,
in my twenties, viscous rayon velvet
patterned from the one in Shillito's

she knew I never could afford.
I kept her sewing shears,
their broken blunted blades.

For Sarah, at 24

The day you were born it snowed fat flakes,
blossoms from green-tipped trees. I wasn't there.
Thirteen is the first birthday in which I
claim some minor role. Tiramisu
with your dad, and later just outside
the restaurant door you smiled your closed mouth,
hide your braces smile when I welcomed you
to your teens. That's how I remember it,
city trees budding above the sidewalks,
you skipping on ahead. I loved those years
that followed, you beside me as I drove.
That's when you'd talk to me. My eyes
on the road; every now and then I'd catch
a sideways glimpse of girl, her life unfurling.

and I've learned to make the words
invisible, the way the eye
behind the camera panning the room
keeps the doorway to her back.
We are all in the room,
no matter what door we entered.
We call the room longing;
we are in it together,
alone.

GRANDMOTHER QUESTIONS IN THIS TIME
OF SOCIAL DISTANCE

How would you describe the scent
of a newborn baby?
Salt and blood,
the woman-slick just begun to dry?
Is it days or weeks until
she's milk and powder,
soap and wipes to clean away the slick
that comes from inside her own self now,
coiled worm of bowels?
Briefly she'll smell of dryer sheets
with names like natural and fresh pine.
Other times it must be
formula dribbled and dried.
What words for all that rises
from deep in the small
caverns of her body?
To me now she is only screen,
face smooth or scrunched,
no whiff of flesh
drifting from my phone.
When finally I can breathe her in,
will that make her any more mine?

First Memory of Pleasure

Riding the long lean horse
of my father's jostling leg, the air
within in my narrow chest released
in ragged bursts of
    ah
  ah
 ah
rattling the downward
slope of bones as I
shake free the last
shard of breath
before pulling it all back
in miraculously whole—
  again,
    again,
        again

THE BLESSING

If you are going to die, why don't you do it all at once and not this little bit of dying every day.
> —Participant at a Dementia Caregiver Workshop

But Mother, it is that bit of you, that stuttering spark
only those bent close enough can see, lighting
the dark around the you I never would have
known had death blazed full and hot
and gone, no charred pieces left
to quietly burn throughout
our bundled days,
the bellow of my
breath against
your skin.

REFLECTION

The old sycamore
overhanging the pond—
how the light on its large, unlovely leaves,
mottled lace by late summer,
reflects not from above
but below,
undersides glowing
with sun mirrored upwards.
How, for an hour or two in the morning,
there is this geometric miracle
witnessed only by me
and anyone else who walks the gravel road
from the retreat center to this lake
named Mary for her statue in the middle,
where I sit, year after year,
trying to find a poem.
There was the year
I stomped the perimeter
trailing a chain of tobacco smoke and fury,
the year of gratitude, too many years
of tears, the year I let go.
Sometimes I think
I am the only thing that changes here.
Then I remember, two summers or more,
Mary lay with the fish at the bottom of her pond,
only to rise again,
aided by what complicated contraption
no one ever said. Soon,
I'll rise too,
on my still sturdy legs,
no closer to knowing light's trajectory,
no farther away.

You can't imagine everything that's in the sky…
—Henri Michaux, "I Am Writing to You from a Far-Off Country"

All day has been about the weather and you. This morning's snowfall thought itself more than it was. Soft down to bristled gray by noon. Then sun and blue, then not. It's not as if this is metaphor for us, though you (who once I was) are silk tailored to the bone, and I (who you become) will lie in bed some mornings trying to remember when it was my body loosened from itself. Counting the folds. Here is what I want you to know: most days—today—I think myself more beautiful than you ever did. You would not believe the way I dance, my husband's hand against the bone the wing would unfold from, should I ever decide to fly.

Things I Would Never Say in a Poem

I love you. I love you more. I love you to the moon and back without at least a whiff of rocket fuel and powdered Tang for the journey. And too, I would have said that Tang would never be in any poem of mine, but there it is. The way my dead mother a lifetime ago plopped the top from a jar of it onto a lidless orange teapot because it fit. The way my husband every morning of our marriage states the moreness of his love with such conviction we were five years in, at least, before it dawned on me the phrase had not originated with him. And dawn without a streak of orange scratched through blueblack sky? Not in my poem. This poem, though, has its own way of saying what it wants to, of taking any old thing and not even trying to make it new. It's not a competition. My husband says that too, and so I let him win. That's how much I love you, I say.

NOSTALGIA

yes, but for the oddest things. Faint whiff
of gas around the stovetop burner's
dim flame, its harvest gold a duskier hue
than the carpet in the only other room,
that second-floor backstairs apartment,
Kanawha Street, Beckley, West Virginia,
1977, where I lay face down,
some nights, my wailing hushed and awkward.
See how my elbows flail as I bang empty
hands into the musty shag. Some part
of me already hovering to observe this self,
her story half-written in my head. The myth
of her begun to rise, wolf moon a crescent
out the window where I'd soon sit up to write.

III.

LITTLE WREN'S SONG

Phoebe said he was too cool
to warm the bed of a girl like me
past summer. I told him that.
He bit off a laugh that wasn't funny.
Said Phoebe was a slag. Said not
to wallow in her bitter mud. Said,

come here, little wren, and let me
kiss you. What else could I do?
His eyes a blue-bruised sky. A girl
like me she's got to fly before she
makes a nest. That's what I told him.
Not then, of course, his mouth against

the curve a throat makes, head thrown
back as if to sing. He never wavered from me.
Black buffed leathers make a girl believe she
has a tougher boy than he knows himself
to be. Even after, all his mournful chatter
rocking south toward me on the postal train.

For Sarah, on the Eve of Her Wedding

The day I married your father
I took you with me to the makeup artist,
remember? You and your friend
both sat in the backseat and all that day
you wore the sunglasses I'd bought you,
though the sky was the same dull gray
as week-old snow,
taking them off only in the Meeting House,
after your dad insisted,

since, miracle of miracles
and despite your braces,
you'd agreed to sing the "minutes" song from *Rent*,
the one it took
five hundred twenty-five thousand six hundred
renderings of at least, to finally bore you.

That year you measured in weddings,
your father's, your mother's.

I measured the years
I had with you
in Tuesdays, Thursdays,
alternate weekends, Chipotle, pad thai,
trips to the mall for endless Pink
and Forever21
until you were
too old.

Thank you for saying I looked pretty
that day. All that make-up!
Whatever was I thinking?
And for those years we filled
like an overstuffed suitcase.
For every minute we had.

Two girls coming out of the underwear store stopped on the sidewalk, in the window behind them a couple of pieces of elasticized lace pulled up over a plastic crotch, and the one girl said to the other, "It was literally a contradiction, I mean it, not even a figurative one, it was a literal contradiction." And I stopped too, by the outdoor adventure store, pretending to look at the hiking boots on the footless, headless mannequin, trying to think up a figurative contradiction. I mean, people pay me money, sometimes, to point out the difference between what's right there in front of them, or could be, and the unseen river that silvers through our dreams, but for the life of me, figuratively speaking, if that torso had had a smoking gun in its cold hand, pointing it at me, I could not have said what it was.

Dear Poem

Where you are,
the humming silence.
Above, a blunt-edged cloud
smudges the blue.
Nothing in need of dusting.
Here, I pry my sentences
apart, begin again. The air
smells of last night's cauliflower.
I wish you were here.

BLOCKING THE DEAD

(for Leslie, whose hacked email address lives on, though she does not)

It seems unnecessarily cruel
like locking a closed window
between a moth and the lamp's pale flame,
and I can't help but think,
maybe, if she were alive, she would
have me click to be amazed,
open my bank account to royalty,
enlarge my penis,
take the years from around my eyes.
It has been years,
but there she is,
a joyful noise in my inbox,
Beloved,
I await your reply.

While Googling Adrienne Rich the Internet Gives Me Adrienne Barbeau, Known for Her Two Enormous Talents

"No one was even listening to me.
They were just watching my breasts precede me."

Storm

I dreamed you here
one night   you were knocking,
you were knocking at the door
I opened
       jagged bolt
of thunder   lightning
       tattooed mouth to ear
across the one side of your
face all flat planes   sharp angles
like the door
you walked in and I said
       (no   not said)
I cried   am I dreaming am I
dreaming
dreaming you said
yes
and kissed me deep
as I stayed
sleeping
in my dream of doors that open
to the mouths of poets
       no
one poet   you
who put your tongue
where mine was   storm
of your mouth into mine
awake now
        what
would you have me say

Story

I never understood the story my mother liked to tell
to company, how when Grandpa's daddy, Felix,
died that thin night, October 31, up on his mountain,
the animals all threw a fit. The scream of mountain lions,
wolves and bears howling
whatever kind of clamor wolves and bears make.
The next day tracks led to his cabin door.

My mother told it better. I was a town kid.
What did I know of wild?
She said he was a hunter and I asked,
were they happy he was dead? No, she said,
they were showing him their honor.
But why? My favorite question.

I liked the story of how when it was time
for Dellie, the least one, to marry,
Felix sent word out and the men came, hats in hand.
He had them toss those hats into the open fire,
sent the girl home with the one whose didn't burn.
That story I understood. Like in all the tales,
woman is the prize
for whatever man or beast outsmarts the king.

My mother loved her grandpa
more than I loved mine.
He was the tallest in any picture,
though we only had the one, holding his Bible,
his wife Rebecca in a flowered dress down to her ankles.
She died.
It was his replacement wife that narrowed Mom's eyes,
the one who hid the peppermints
when she'd call down the holler

for the kids to come and do her chores,
after she got Dellie out of the way.
I'd been read that story too,
the evil second queen.

It wasn't till later that I learned to read myself
and do some math. Dellie was 13
when she was carried off to be somebody's bride.
Thirteen, the age that I was too,
the first tracks to and from my door.

THOSE BIG-BONED, BLACK-HAIRED
COUNTRY BOYS

who sat in back rows of the yellow bus—exhaust stink, switchback
turns, rattle of torn-up benches—who tattooed their arms
like carving sticks of wood with ink pens and red pocket knives
that coal camp year before my father gave in to my sister's tears
at the indignity of buses, and drove us in his hatchback Datsun
to the school in town where we belonged, not up some holler road,
where runoff from the mine smelled like mayonnaise
in the creek my brother liked to wade until we came home.

What am I saying? That place was not home.
But when my father got a college job again,
and us a town with sidewalks,
those big-boned, black-haired country boys
went with me in my mind. Their arms like ropes
they threw around each other's shoulders.
Their downturned eyes.

Boys like that, they never even looked at me
until they did, two years gone by,
boys like them at half-time in the county high school gym,
the Bobcats down by six—

      I am 13,
      the lift and curve of flesh around my bones.
      Boys call me and I turn.
      My father's hand against my nape
      guides me back to way up in the bleachers.
      Boys follow with their country eyes.

My mother would have told me, had she seen,
"You don't know what it is you're wanting."
And it is true, the other way as well,
I had not known I wanted
what I did not know,
until I did.

Me Too

Because I, too,
was once 13,
because I did not
k[no]w
I was too
beautiful, because
he could,
because everybody knew
this flesh was what defined me,
because men will be
boys, because I was
a perk of the job,
because
I only wanted
to be seen.

This Is the Poem That Has Been Staring at You for Some Time Now

Remember the night you saw yourself
in the mirror the other side of the bar,
Arnold's, 1985, framed between the bottles,
and you were slapped by
your own loveliness, unloved?
That was the poem.
It wanted to ask you
what it was you were
so afraid of.
Now it thinks it knows
the only perfect poem
is the one you would have written
then, and then is never now,
and now is always too soon.
Tonight in the mirror you want
to slap that girl's other cheek,
if you only knew where she was,
wake her up to her life.
But the only perfect happiness
is the one you don't know
is yours.

Letter to Myself, 15

It's Time, of course. (Is it the same where you are?)
—Henri Michaux, "I Am Writing to You from a Far-Off Country"

For so many years you kept all the letters they sent you, boxes in the attic weighting the air as we dreamed. Now I choose whose words to keep near. If we are skin, you are peeled bark of sycamore long gone from me. If we are bone, you are always mine. This letter I write is your own.

INTERVIEW

Anyone who wishes to write the truth must overcome at least five difficulties.
—Bertolt Brecht

1. (1990)

Let's go back to 1975.
Pauletta, you're...
      caught stitched at the seam of the mountain. I felt real trapped.
Pauletta, you're...
      a loose thread,
leaving and coming back...
      The truth is it was a lot looser than that.
Go on.
      The truth is my life has been a constant moving between.
Let's go back...
      Over time things mend and it's not as if you can't see the cracks.
to 1975.
      People were beginning to believe
      they could do something about the powers
      that had affected them all their lives.
So lead me through some lives here.
      They were looking to their history.
      The pressures from the outside were kindling a strength
Let's go back...
      to find a place where people have a voice,
      where they never had one before.
to 1975.
      The truth is what we saw wasn't really there.
      There are other ways to measure. The truth
Pauletta,
      is I think it took me longer to find what didn't fit.
      As it was, what I chose to do was to leave and to stay gone.
you're 15.
      The truth is I haven't written in that way for many years.

2. (2020)

You are trying to remember what trapped meant to you then. The mountains pushing in and how the only voice you had was typed on the page. You lived two lives. The mirror cracked, and you somewhere outside it, watching. Remember? You couldn't pass a glass without looking for your own reflection, see your hand move up to touch your own mouth.   **Shh.**   What?   What did you want to tell me? There is the history on the typed page. You were a girl who wrote yourself into a woman. There is the history of the body.   ***Shhh! We don't talk. We don't talk about...***   Remember? His hand pushing down your head your mouth to where it was made you a woman. You are trying to remember trapped, the girl you want to strip away, the soft slough of her useless to you now, the woman all hard planes, a hundred shattered shards hold girl, behind her, mountains all around and pushing. There is a road, but the road is still inside you. For all your black typed words trapped on the page, you have not found it yet. You are trying. Remember.

3. (1975)

```
reading womanpoems,
my fingers
reach wildly.
paper!
pen!
underneath the nails,
i feel them,
womanlines,
screaming
for release.
quick!
before i
bite them away.
                p.h.
```

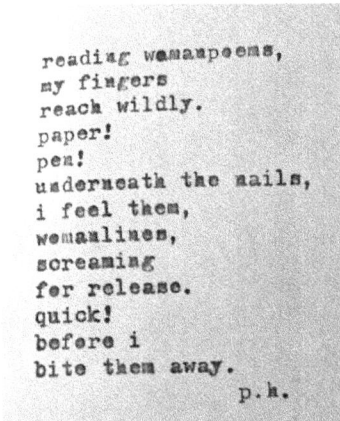

You were 15 when you wrote that poem/

when i wrote this poem, i was 15

I haven't written in that way for many years.

4.

Let's go back, but not all the way back.

5.

15 years after I was 15,
I was interviewed about being an Appalachian poet,
which I wasn't anymore. Not then.
A poet, I mean.
          Let's go back
                    to 1975.
                              Pauletta, you're...
The year before I turned 15, I had sex with a man ten years older.
          (Call it what it was)
Being already a poet, I told it slant,
          (You were raped)
the angle of the mirror cocked
          (*i called it making love*)
so even my eye
could not catch the *i*
of the girl
          (*i called myself a woman*)
I wanted not to be.

Over the years, I wrote myself
out of that girl,
but into silence.

          I haven't written in that way for many years.

I am trying to write her voice back into me.
I am looking to my history.
I am kindling a strength.

          It's not as if you can't see the cracks.

IV.

COMPLICIT (A BRIEF HISTORY)

Stories, like languages,
depend upon patterns
for the forming of words
and for connecting them
in ways that can be understood.
Some words are made
by a process known as
backformation,
a part of a longer word
plied away.
"Complicit," for example,
with its roots, like those of "complicated,"
embedded in the Latin *com/plicare*,
                    together / folded,
came straggling in
around the time my family
staked what little claim we could
here in these Appalachian Mountains
where already the weight
of millions of years of life and death
had folded one into the other
down and down into the seams.
Bituminous coal
appears smooth when first you see it
but look closer and you'll find
many layers in a past
to which we can only be
accomplice.

THEIR WAR ON POVERTY

We never knew ourselves
as they did. We didn't know our faces
and floors should be dirt, our red
brick homes, pink geraniums in pots
along the patio walls should be great-granny's
mud-chinked cabin or a rusted trailer listing
by a pitted road, either way, rows of beans
out back, one for every young'un to hoe.
We didn't know our very names could conjure
photos, black and white in glossy magazines,
our creeks and towns strange stones
rolled against our nation's tongue—
Elkatawa, Hardshell, Keck.
What else did we not know?
That one man pillaring coal
was no different than another
man beneath some other mountain,
that all that matters is black numbers,
row by row in someone else's bank.
We only knew ourselves to be enough
until we weren't,
and then we saw ourselves
packed tight with all the othered ones
who surely in today's America
could only blame
themselves.

Unto the Least of These

Soul crushing. PTSD symptoms showing up in more than half of Children's Services workers.
  —*Cincinnati Enquirer* headline, March 6, 2019

You take it home,
tuck it away,
maybe just a little at first—
the wince she says is maybe from the whupping
last night or the one before
as you buckle up the car seat
in your county-issued van.
The used syringe beside his crusty Sponge Bob bath soap.
Slight whiff of old pee
from the kid who called you Mom the time
you drove him to his 7th foster home that year,
asking, *Why can't I just stay with you?*
Meanwhile your own babies
smell like lavender shampoo,
like Play-Doh, like dryer sheets,
like peanut butter sandwiches
in triangles on a clean plate, crusts cut away,
smell like all they've ever known
is love right now will last forever,
and how do you remember
to keep that love apart—
the kid you tuck beneath her princess comforter,
the kid whose rape at 12 is tucked
between your sternum and ribs
so deep you think you'll bleed to death
if you ever try to pull it out.

To Break a Thing

for Ron Houchin, his story

He said, "We're in the bath, her quick hands
soaping both of us. I turn and see
her wobbling breasts, nipples the color
of clay. I was two—I knew without knowing
that red triangle of groin was a home
I was not to go back to. At fifteen,

"give or take a wasted year or two,
this first lost memory of her
bobbed up to be pushed down
to that place of other broken things—
thrown dishes, toys, their marriage, split
lips from whatever was handy

"when I needed from her more than she had.
By then I was the delinquent
the grandparents she'd dumped me on
at six always knew I'd turn out to be.
She'd got her own place across town
so she could find a new dad for me,

"she said, but when I'd run those night
streets crying from her parents' shriveled
mercies to her closed door she'd just fling
me wild back to the dark I grew to love.
I could break into anything—houses, cars.
We called it joyriding: drive until you

"run it out of gas, leave it empty
where it lands. I broke my ribs,
my shoulder, fingers, toes. I broke

my leg three times—same leg. That last
fall from somebody else's fire escape
is what wholly broke me.

"I landed in a world of books. What else
was there to do, those weeks in traction,
but read and think? I always wonder,
how was it that she knew—
she surely knew—you have to break
a thing to make a new thing from it."

poetry doesn't make you a better person,
and the news that can be found there
is like some gone week's Sunday *Times*
tossed in its clear green wrapper
beneath the neighbor's car.
The one who died
and no one came to find him,
and you didn't knock on his door
when his trashcan of carryout chicken and ribs
sat spilling its own kind of news.
Maybe.
But, oh, to live awhile as marrow
in someone else's bones,
to breathe her breath upon the mirror
held up to your life,
doesn't it make you want
to fling open whatever door you come to,
doesn't it make you want to try?

This Is Not a Drill

It's true I was mostly schooled between bomb threats;
no need to squeeze my big-girl limbs beneath
my ink-scratched wooden desk, scaled
to a generation less fleshy than my own,
and everything bad that happened

happened somewhere else, behind curtains
of iron (which I confused with lungs
made of the same dull metal), to children
whose monthly allowance did not trust in God—
those heathen babies we lit candles for.

My cousin died rocking himself in a cardboard box.
His neck snapped back and I never saw him again.
But even he was a country cousin
with gravel instead of a lawn.

And so I am trying now to squeeze myself
into the shoes of my poetry students, to walk
the crisscross mile of their hallways and stairwells,
wondering who's on the other side of the lockdown door.

One told me no way should they give teachers guns—
you can never tell who's going to snap. Another needed all
the fingers on her one hand to show the times she'd faced a gun
outside her house, the other hand for home.

They really ought to check my backpack, she told me.
I don't know why they think it won't be me.

Postcard from the Dark Woods' Edge

I had wanted to write you a metaphor, branches
bristling the sky, homely as the squat brown brushes

my mother bought from the salesman's catalogue,
one for each of us, our caught strands

as clear a claim on our own as leaves budding
from walnut or oak. But all I can think about

is last night's radio story, the woman whose boyfriend
left her at the ER door, a hairbrush pushed inside her.

This was in Mexico, or maybe down the street.
How the doctor called in the orderlies, the nurses,

even the janitors to sneer at her vagina, misshapen
and torn as a thrown-away grocery bag tangled in the brush.

This story contains graphic descriptions of sexual violence.
Take care of yourself and those near you. On the radio

they call it femicide, men killing women because they can.
I can't decide if giving it a name makes it easier to see.

Above, the gibbous moon is rising pale. We are a planet
hurtling through space. The tips of branches

have thickened with the green that pushes from the inside,
invisible to us until it's not.

I Confess

These days I think too much
about assassination, and let me just say
I have come down against it every time,
swatting it away, a plague-ridden fly

in my otherwise mild and law-abiding imagination,
and I do not accept the legal argument
that targeted killings are a country's form
of self-defense, regardless of whether the target

will ever see the inside of a detention center,
and be faced with deciding, like thousands
of seven-year-olds, should the assigned Mylar blanket
go over or under on the mud-caked concrete floor.

Every time, I rise up on the right side of the question
though I have gone so far as to research the word
from the Arabic, *hashshashin*, the Assassins of Persia,
perhaps so-named for the necessity of getting high

before slipping in the blade. (In private,
some Border Patrol agents consider migrant deaths
a laughing matter; others are succumbing to depression,
anxiety, or substance abuse.)

How, with or without the name, the act
is older than our ability to write it down.
How way back in the Old Testament,
there it was alongside the begetting and begats.

How in the Roman Empire, strangling in the bathtub
was the method of choice for murdering one's king,
while, as you might expect, in Japan it was the sword.
Here in the US we, as always,

prefer the gun, and let me just say,
I do not and will not own one.
I confess only to the image in my mind
of the mongrel dogs of history lapping at the wound.

Saying It

My best allegiances are to the dead.
    — Gwendolyn Brooks

Words form themselves like glass shards in my
mouth, no place to rest my tongue. It's best
to spit them out fast. Hold no fixed allegiances.
Some say the past lives on in us. Some are
wrong. A memory is not a hand cupped to
your sleeping breast. No flame against the
cold. So, say it then. Dead.

MUNDUS NOVUS

300,000 US dead, I read
this morning (old news
by the time you read these words).
This pandemic's
in month nine, fully gestated.
The curve of it ready to pop.
My husband, the historian,
looks across the table at me,
tells me this won't be the last plague
of our lifetime, this won't be the worst.
We're in our sixties now. How much longer
does the next one have to find us?
Twenty, thirty years?
How many of them would we choose
to claim, years not given up to pills and tubes,
the cancer that his mother didn't fight,
the dementia that wrote the ending
of both my parents' stories?
I pick up again the book
that names my New World kin—
Ezekiel, Margaret—
newlywed and not among
300 grisly dead that year,
Jamestown, 1622, settlers
with their own weapons slain,
the Powhatans' wasted dose
of our own medicine
to rid themselves of our encroaching whiteness.
Rapacious is the word
the author gives to my ancestral
plundering of the world
that was not new or ours,
as even now we thrust our will
across this landscape, not unlike the virus
we no longer call *novel*.

STORY

What I'm saying is we've been stitched to this place a long time, and this place has always been complicated. Frayed seams are mended, ripped again. The stories I tell you now, embroidered patches, other lives to mine. So here I sit, trying to piece a poem from my maternal line, a row of names, like the begats: Ebesine carried Elizabeth carried Eveline carried Sarah carried Etta carried Larnie carried me. Because we all know that most of what gets written is his story. Even their names uncarved, as on the stone that does not mark my father's mother's grave beneath rough grass and bramble at the cemetery's edge. Pauline. But right there on the internet is my first New World grandmother, Margaret Dauson, or Dawson, Jamestown, 1621. It doesn't get more American than that, with the plundering and the massacres, the first Africans enslaved. At 24 or 25, she left England as "a good and faithfull servant," a mail-order bride before there was mail, to be wed for a price of 150 pounds of tobacco leaves. Her journey not made chained in the belly of the great white wooden *Warwick*, like those others erased, my DNA traces Cameroon, Congo, the southern Bantu. I have no claim to those I carry. Margaret outlived three husbands and left to my many-great-grandfather two households with all moveables and unmoveables, including one yearling and heifer, one Negro woman, and all their increase, to be his and his heirs forever. Nine generations later, Leslie County, Kentucky, Nancy Lewis in her Civil War widow appeal was down to one cow, two hogs, borrowed a mule to plow. At least nobody owned anyone anymore. My mother, when she died, owned the family graveyard though she had lost the deed and made us promise not to plant her there. What I'm saying? I come from what's sewn too deep in the seams to be picked out clean.

These Stories I Tell You Now

Ebesine carried
Elizabeth carried
Eveline carried
Sarah carried
Etta carried
Larnie carried
Pauletta carried…

carried…

reader
breathe these lines
as I breathe now
stop here
where my hand
stays

begin again
release of words
my breath
into yours
carry
me

To You

We need all the mothers we can get,
I once was fond of saying,
and I was talking about me, then,
mothering all my borrowed girls—
the one who wrote me at the end of class,
shy as pencil strokes, "I pretend,
sometimes, you are my real mother";
the one who nested in our love seat,
silent but for clicks below her screen,
Tuesdays, Thursdays, alternate weekends,
until her father drove her to her real home
on the other side of town,
as decreed.
I didn't know you
back when I pretended longing was enough
to make a girl my own.
I admit it now.
I need all the daughters
I can find. The grown ones,
fine web of lines around kind mother eyes,
who love me for my longing,
daughters who are mothers
to my words.

Letter to Myself, 15

I am writing to you from the end of the world.
—Henri Michaux, "I Am Writing to You from a Far-Off Country"

I want to tell you how, in time, everything shows on the skin. Today, turning my wrist to bite an apple, I saw a new ridge at the base of my palm. A gentle rise of loosened flesh, not like the sharp slashed mountains where you, in my mind, your only home, remain. Think instead of farmland, river basin, sloped pastures, plowed fields. O, you smooth girl. Broken only by the sharp protrusion of bone you were so proud of—ankle, knee, hip, steep pitch of pelvic cage above the valley. The ridge of ribs. You hungered away the softness. Your power lay not in the just-ripe plums of breast but in the knob between them. What have I done with you? What did you do to me? There is a small scar, a distant lightning bolt, on my right wrist slashed all those years ago by the impatience of the left thumb's jagged nail. Every time I see its raised white welt, I think of the one who hurt me open then, his love—we'll call it that—a scalpel to the other scars you once lifted your body to receive, now invisible beneath the bone. Did you believe if you could hide what did not heal, the hurt would cease to matter? But we are made of matter, girl. And now this body you have left me to begins to show your leaving. Think deer track through the fallow winter field where every step in thawing ground is visible. And I am trying to love this land, mine now to tend.

NOTES

"Letter to Myself, 15," a series, contains epigraphs from Henri Michaux's "I Am Writing to You from a Far-Off Country," translation by John Hayes.

"Dirt" contains definitions from *Reconnaissance Soil Survey: Fourteen Counties in Eastern Kentucky*, USDA, Series 1962, No. 1.

"For Beauty" includes an epigraph and lines from Don West's "Harlan Portraits." Growing conditions description is from www.wildflower.org (Lady Bird Johnson Wildflower Center, the University of Texas at Austin).

"Some Facts About Home" is a found poem using lines from Wikipedia and a San Francisco State University 2003 course website featuring student Charlotte Ely's "The Biogeography of the Writing Spider."

"Story" (Have I ever told you my mother) is in response to the poem "Forgiveness" by Erica Manto-Paulson.

"Storm" is for the late poet Aralee Strange.

"This Is the Poem That Has Been Staring at You for Some Time Now" is a line in a poem by Mark Flanigan in *Journeyman's Lament*.

"Interview" includes phrases from a 1990 interview by Chris Green for his dissertation on the Southern Appalachian Writers Cooperative. At 15, I was an early member. Most of Section 1 is taken from this interview, as is the epigraph from Brecht's "Writing the Truth: Five Difficulties," which Chris quoted from an early SAWC brochure.

"Complicit (A Brief History)" draws from "A Brief History of 'Complicit'" on the *Merriam Webster* website and from the Kentucky Coal Education website.

"Their War on Poverty" is so named because that national project, begun in the mid-1960s, implanted many of the stereotypes about Appalachia that are still common today.

"To Break a Thing" is a collaboration with Ron Houchin and Leigh Cheak, inspired by a workshop led by Rebecca Gayle Howell.

The parenthetical in "I Confess" is from *The Atlantic*, July 3, 2019.

"Saying It" is a "golden shovel" using a line from Gwendolyn Brooks' poem "Mentors."

"Story" (What I'm saying is) contains my family connection to Margaret Dauson (or Dawson) Wroughton, as researched by the late Appalachian scholar Danny Miller. Thanks, Danny, and sorry it has taken me this long to follow up.

Acknowledgments

My gratitude to the editors of the following publications in which versions of these poems appeared, some with different titles, and especially to Robert and Elizabeth Murphy of Dos Madres Press, beloved friends to me and my poems.

Anthology of Appalachian Writers, XIII (Shepherd University, 2021): "Letter to Myself, 15" (Listen, girl), "Story" (I never understood), and "Postcard from the Dark Woods' Edge"

Appalachian Journal: "Complicit (A Brief History)," "The Road," "Some Facts About Home," and "Their War on Poverty"

Change Seven: "Story" (My mother said) and "Letter to Myself, 15" (I want to tell you how)

Cutleaf Journal: "Things I Would Never Say in a Poem" and "So maybe it's true"

Friend (Dos Madres Press, 2020): "Story" (I don't mean to be ungrateful), "Story" (Have I ever told you my mother), "Perhaps all my poems begin with I want," and "Grandmother Questions in This Time of Social Distance"

Heartwood Literary Magazine: "Their War on Poverty"

If Only They Were Hungrier They Would Swallow Me Whole (LexPoMo Anthology, 2019): "This Is the Poem That Has Been Staring at You for Some Time Now"

I Thought I Heard a Cardinal Sing, Ohio's Appalachian Voices (Sheila-Na-Gig Editions, 2022): "Poem Written While Contemplating a Newly Dug Southern Kentucky Grave" and "Pattern"

Lexington Poetry Month website: "For Sarah, at 24," "Joy," "Poem Written While Contemplating a Southern Kentucky Grave," "For Sarah, on the Eve of Her Wedding," "Grandmother Questions in This Time of

Social Distance," and "This Is the Poem That Has Been Staring at You for Some Time Now"

Literary Accents: "The Heartbreak Tree," "Me Too," "The Stepmother's Lament," and "Little Wren's Song"

Molecule Magazine: "While Googling Adrienne Rich the Internet Gives Me Adrienne Barbeau, Known for Her Two Enormous Talents"

The New Verse News: "Mundus Novus"

Northern Appalachia Review: "This Is Not a Drill" and "Saying It"

Panoply: "Those big-boned, black-haired country boys"

Peauxdunque Review: "It snows across the mountains"

Pegasus: "Postcard from Age 60" (Kentucky State Poetry Society, 2020 Chaffin/Kash Award)

Persimmon: "Letter to Myself, 15" (All day has been about the weather and you)

Pine Mountain Sand & Gravel: "Unto the Least of These" and "Interview"

Psaltery & Lyre: "Story" (I don't mean to be ungrateful) and "Reflection"

Pudding Magazine: "Story" (Have I ever told you my mother)

Rattle, Poets Respond: "I Confess"

Roanoke Review: "At the Lifestyle Center"

Sequestrum: "Blocking the Dead" and "Storm"

Sheila-Na-Gig: "Dirt" and "The Road"

Soren Lit: "Home Is the Place Where, When You Have to Go There, You Only Think About How to Get Out" and "For Beauty"

Still: The Journal: "Home Is the Place Where, When You Have to Go There, You Only Think About How to Get Out" (Fall 2019 Poetry Contest Winner), "Returned Addressee Unknown," "Morning, Loretto Motherhouse, Late November," "Complicit (A Brief History)," "To Break a Thing," and "Story" (What I'm saying is)

Thimble Literary Magazine: "Joy"

Vox Populi: "The Road," "Joy," and "The Stepmother's Lament"

What Things Cost: an anthology for the people (University Press of Kentucky, 2022): "I Confess"

Women Speak (Sheila-Na-Gig Editions): "Postcard from Age 60," "This Is the Poem That Has Been Staring at You for Some Time Now," "Interview," and "Letter to Myself, 15" (I want to tell you how, in time)

WORDS (Thomas More University Literary Journal): "For Sarah, on the Eve of Her Wedding" and "This Is the Poem That Has Been Staring at You for Some Time Now"

Writing in a Woman's Voice: "Story" (My mother said)

Thank you to the amazing poet Alison Luterman who read and commented upon this manuscript as I revised it, and to Dale Marie Prenatt, my goddaughter and fellow poet, for her careful reading and encouragement (and title suggestion). I am also indebted to Linda Parsons, Madville Publishing's poetry editor, a stellar poet herself, who provided generous editorial assistance.

This book would not exist without my beloved teacher and poet Rebecca Gayle Howell, who mentored me throughout the writing of these poems and the early development of this manuscript. And, of course, this book would, quite literally, not exist without Madville Publishing, mothered by the fabulous Kim Davis. I need all the mothers—and daughters—I can get, and I cherish each one.

About the Author

Pauletta Hansel is a poet, memoirist, and teacher who is author of eight previous poetry collections, including *Friend, Coal Town Photograph*, and *Palindrome*, winner of the 2017 Weatherford Award for Appalachian Poetry. Her writing has been widely anthologized and featured in print and online journals, including *Oxford American, Rattle, The Writer's Almanac, American Life in Poetry, Verse Daily, Appalachian Journal, Appalachian Review, Cincinnati Review*, and *Still: The Journal*, among others. Pauletta was Cincinnati's first Poet Laureate, 2016-2018, and the Public Library of Cincinnati and Hamilton County's 2022 Writer-in-Residence.